ALL YOU NEI
ABOUT PLAYING
DISC GOLF
FOR BEGINNERS

Beyond The Court, Simplified Step By
Step Practical Knowledge Guide To
Learn And Master How To Play Disc
Golf From Scratch

Travis Bowden

Disclaimer:

This book is a work of fiction/non-fiction, and any resemblance to actual persons, living or dead, or actual events is purely coincidental.

The views expressed in this book are solely those of the author and do not necessarily reflect the views of any organization, company, or individual.

The author would like to clarify that they are not in any endorsement deal with any organization, company, or individual mentioned in this book.

Any references to products, services, or entities are made for literary or informational purposes and do not constitute an endorsement or promotion.

Readers are advised to consider this work as a creative endeavor, and the author disclaims any responsibility for consequences arising from any actions or decisions based on the content of this book.

Any opinions expressed within are the author's own and should not be construed as professional advice.

Contents

ABOUT THE BOOK:

"Flight Paths and Fairways" offers a thorough examination of disc golf, covering everything from basic principles to sophisticated tactics, and transports readers on a fascinating voyage through the dynamic world of the game. This book is your go-to resource since it offers a plethora of knowledge to both novice and expert players.

Introduction: Take a deep dive into the world of disc golf to learn about its history, development, and the pure joy it offers players around.

Discover the fundamentals of Disc Golf: Gain an understanding of the many disc types and become proficient in the fundamental rules and methods that form the basis of this thrilling sport.

Rules and Etiquette: Learn about the disc golf rules and etiquette to help you navigate the fairways with confidence. This will guarantee that players of all skill levels have a seamless and pleasurable time on the course.

Disc Golf Courses: Discover the many environments that are home to disc golf courses and how course design affects gameplay and improves the player experience overall.

Methods and Throws: Learn the keys to getting accuracy, distance, and control with each toss as you delve into the artistry of disc golf throws and techniques.

Strategies & Game Play: Improve your performance by using strategic insights, experimenting with different play styles, managing the course, and changing the course to meet new difficulties.

Disc Golf Community: Get involved in the lively Disc Golf community and learn about the events, competitions, and friendships that make this sport a welcoming and social pastime.

Fitness and Conditioning: Learn about the physical requirements of disc golf and investigate fitness and conditioning strategies designed to improve your power, dexterity, and endurance while playing.

Discover the tales, turning points, and significant individuals who have molded disc golf into the sport it is today as you immerse yourself in its rich culture and history.

In conclusion, as you approach the last hole, consider your disc golf adventure and welcome the feelings of achievement, friendship, and personal development that this distinctive sport offers. "Flight Paths and Fairways" is an invitation to immerse yourself in the wonder of Disc Golf rather than just a guidebook.

Overview

Disc golf is a fast-rising sport that blends traditional golf components with the art of flying disc throwing. Disc golf, which is played on a course with nine or eighteen "holes," has become more and more well-liked due to its accessibility, low cost, and wide variety of players. This article explores the history, objectives, and reasons disc golf has become a popular pastime for many people, delving into the subtleties of the game.

The history of disc golf

The inception of disc golf dates back to the 1960s, when a few people began modifying the conventional golf rules to allow for the pitching of flying discs. The sport of disc golf was formalized in 1975 with the establishment of the first recognized course. Disc golf has changed over time, with different courses having different layouts and levels of difficulty. The establishment of the Professional Disc Golf Association (PDGA) in 1976 added to the sport's expansion and standardization.

Disc golf courses can be found in parks, woods, or other open spaces, offering players a varied and unspoiled environment. Players must finish each of the holes—which are often made of metal baskets—in the fewest throws feasible. The usage of various discs, each intended for a certain function, gives the game an additional degree of skill and strategy.

Goals and Purpose of the Book

This investigation aims to present a thorough introduction to disc golf, including its background, strategies, regulations, and the distinct culture that has grown up around the game. This book endeavors to be an invaluable tool for all players, be they seasoned veterans seeking to hone their craft or novices eager to grasp the fundamentals.

The gaming mechanics are only one aspect of the book's scope. It explores the cerebral components of disc golf, such as concentration, tactics, and the friendship that is developed between players. The book also examines the development of disc golf as a professional sport, showcasing important competitions, well-known players, and the sport's growing international appeal.

Why Play Disc Golf?

Disc golf's ease of use and low entrance barrier make it appealing to a wide range of people. It's less equipment-intensive than traditional golf; all you need is a set of discs. Because the sport is informal, individuals of different ability levels can enjoy it with one another, which promotes inclusivity.

Disc golf's emphasis on outdoor activities and exercise is one of its main draws. Players interact with the course on a mental and physical level as they navigate a variety of terrains. The activity offers a fun substitute for more traditional types of exercise while promoting a healthy lifestyle.

Disc golf also has a special social component. A lot of players value the sense of community and camaraderie that comes with playing the sport.

Players can meet, exchange stories, and create enduring connections through local leagues, events, and tournaments.

Disc golf is more than just a game; it's a thriving sport that continues to draw people from all over the world as well as a demanding physical activity and community. We invite both new and experienced players to embark with us on this adventure into the exciting world of flying discs and difficult courses as we examine the various aspects of disc golf in this book.

CHAPTER ONE

DISC GOLF'S FUNCTIONALITY

A popular and quickly expanding sport, disc golf mixes features of regular golf with the use of a frisbee. The goal is to finish each hole on the course in the fewest throws possible. Disc golf is well-known for being easily accessible, needing little in the way of equipment, and offering players of all abilities a fun outdoor experience.

Meaning And History

Disc golf, sometimes referred to as Frisbee golf, first appeared in the 1960s and has since developed into a reputable sport.

Like traditional golf, the goal is to finish a course with the fewest number of tosses. From being a popular recreational activity, the sport has developed into a competitive endeavor with sanctioned competitions for players at all skill levels.

The Goal Of The Game

In disc golf, the main objective is to finish a course—which usually consists of nine or eighteen holes—in the fewest number of throws possible. Every hole has a target, commonly a metal basket with dangling chains, and a defined starting position. An additional degree of difficulty is added to the game when players traverse a variety of terrains, including hills, open fields, and wooded places.

Essential Tools

Disc golf is accessible to a broad spectrum of players due to its low equipment requirements. The disc, which comes in a variety of sizes and forms, is the most important piece of equipment. For example, putters are used for short, precise strokes, drivers are used for long-distance throws and mid-range discs are used for intermediate distances. The discs' flight characteristics are intended to resemble those of conventional golf clubs.

Disc Types

In disc golf, there are three primary kinds of discs: putters, mid-range discs, and drivers. Putters are used for precise, short-range shots, while drivers are made for the longest distances. Mid-range discs provide a compromise between distance and accuracy. Success in disc golf depends on knowing the traits of each type and selecting the appropriate disc for the given circumstance.

Disc Flight Classifications

Flight ratings are a set of four numbers that are applied to discs to represent their speed, glide, turn, and fade. Players can select discs that best suit their throwing style and ability level with the use of these ratings. The disc's initial velocity is represented by speed, its capacity to sustain altitude is measured by glide, its propensity to curve during flight is indicated by turn, and its fade at the end of flight is described by fade.

17

CHAPTER TWO

ADDITIONAL REQUIRED EQUIPMENT

Players can improve their disc golfing experience by using a variety of accessories in addition to discs. Throughout a round, a disc golf bag comes in handy for carrying many discs and frequently has pockets for food and water bottles.

In addition to using towels to dry discs and maintain optimum grip, many players find that wearing supportive and comfortable footwear is essential for handling a variety of terrains.

Disc golf is an energetic, all-inclusive sport that blends outdoor leisure, strategy, and accuracy. For players of all ages and ability levels, disc golf offers a distinctive and entertaining experience, whether it is played socially with friends or competitively in sanctioned competitions.

Guidelines And Etiquette

Disc golf is a fast-rising sport that blends traditional golf aspects with the accuracy and dexterity of disc throwing. A fun and fair game depends on players knowing the rules and manners.

Basic Guidelines for Play

The goal of disc golf is to finish a course in the fewest number of throws feasible. Usually, a course has nine or eighteen holes, each with a different par score. To begin, players must tee off from a specific area and move toward the objective, which is often a metal basket with chains hanging from it. A smooth game requires an understanding of the general principles of play, which include how to navigate the course and calculate scoring.

Tee Displaces

Every hole starts with a tee throw. A tee pad or other marker often designates the specified tee location from which players must toss their discs. The kind of throw, the disc choice, and the tactic used on tee throws all have a big effect on how well a player performs overall. Gaining accuracy and distance with tee throws requires understanding the rules and technique.

Throws On The Fairway

Fairway throws become increasingly important as players progress through the course to get over obstacles and reach the objective. To clear obstacles like trees, shrubs, and elevation changes, players must strike a balance between power and accuracy when making a fairway throw. A player's effectiveness on the course is influenced by their comprehension of the fairway throw regulations and their ability to practice the appropriate techniques.

Positioning

Putting is the last step in finishing a hole. With as few throws as possible, players try to get their discs into the intended basket.

There are particular guidelines for stance, foot placement, and putt completion when playing putt golf. Gaining proficiency in the skill of putting is necessary to regularly score highly in disc golf.

Rating

The number of throws needed to finish a hole determines the score in disc golf. After the course, the player with the fewest throws wins.

It is essential to comprehend the disc golf scoring system, which includes terms like pars, bogeys, and birdies, to monitor and compare performance.

Etiquette and Conduct Guidelines

Disc golfers are expected to abide by a code of behavior and etiquette in addition to the game's rules.

All participants will have a courteous and pleasurable experience thanks to these standards.

In Motion

One of the main tenets of the code of conduct is respect for the course and its surroundings. It is expected of players not to trash, cause damage to the course, or interfere with the surrounding environment. Practicing good course etiquette helps keep disc golf courses sustainable in the long run.

Having Conversations With Other Players

Playing disc golf is a social activity, and having fun with other players is a big part of it.

On the course, a pleasant and welcoming atmosphere is created by being polite, keeping quiet during opponents' throws, and keeping an optimistic outlook.

Play's Tempo

To maintain a smooth game flow and prevent undue delays for other players, players must play at an efficient speed. Gamers should move quickly between shots, be aware of their time, and make thoughtful selections. Everyone's experience on the course is enhanced when there is consideration for the pace of play.

CHAPTER THREE

DISC GOLF COURSES

A popular sport, disc golf is played on a course with many target baskets and characteristics of both regular golf and frisbee. The disc golf courses are different in terms of layout, setting, and level of difficulty, providing players with a wide variety of playing experiences. Players of all skill levels must comprehend the various facets of disc golf courses.

Course Types

Disc golf courses are available in a variety of styles to suit players' tastes and ability levels. The two main types of courses are temporary and permanent.

Ongoing Classes

Permanent disc golf courses are pre-made designs that have tees, targets, and other infrastructure in place. These courses are meant to be a permanent feature of the recreational options available in a community, giving nearby disc golfers a dependable and steady playing surface. Permanent courses frequently have difficult holes, varied topography, and extras like benches and tee signs.

Short-Term Courses

Temporary disc golf courses are constructed for particular occasions or events. These courses could make use of already-existing park areas or be created especially for transient play.

In situations like tournaments, festivals, or other events where setting up a permanent course would not be feasible, temporary courses are frequently used.

Course Structure

A key component of disc golf that affects the playing experience overall is course design. Every hole's layout is meticulously planned by designers, who consider the course's flow, the natural landscape characteristics, and the difficulty level balance.

To test players' abilities, well-designed courses have a combination of open and wooded regions, different distances, and inventive hole placements.

Pars and Holes

Disc golf courses are made up of several holes, each of which has a specified par, or the number of throws required for a skilled player to finish the hole. The length of a hole can vary from short and easy to lengthy and difficult, so players must plan their throws to get past obstacles and hit the target with the fewest shots.

Barriers and Surface

Disc golf courses are distinguished by their varied terrain and presence of hazards. The game is made more difficult and exciting by the presence of trees, bushes, water dangers, and height changes.

Competent players have to modify how they throw to get around obstacles and make use of the course's natural features.

Safety Points To Remember

Playing disc golf requires utmost safety for both participants and spectators. Because safety is a top priority when designing a course, holes are strategically placed to reduce the possibility of discs colliding with other players or park visitors. A safe playing environment is enhanced by appropriate signage, teeing places that are assigned, and well-defined pathways connecting holes. To provide a fun and safe disc golf experience, players are also urged to be aware of their surroundings, other players, and park regulations.

CHAPTER FOUR

METHODS AND STRIKES:

Players use a range of throws and strategies in disc golf to effectively navigate the course. The secret to success is learning the various throws and knowing when to employ them about the course's unique challenges.

Hold And Posture:

The basis for a successful throw in disc golf is a solid grip and stance. Players frequently utilize either a fan grip or a power grip, depending on the circumstance. To provide the most power and control, the stance calls for precise foot placement and balance.

Throw Backhand:

In disc golf, one of the most important moves is the backhand throw. To create spin and distance, one must rotate the hand while holding the disc with the back of the hand facing the target.

Accuracy and consistency in backhand throws depend on an understanding of their mechanics.

Mechanisms:

Disk golf throw mechanics include things like follow-through, spin rate, and release angle. It takes repetition and practice to get these mechanics just right for a throwing motion that is reliable and repeatable.

Suggestions For Enhancement:

Disc golfers can concentrate on particular areas to improve their game. This could entail honing the grip, improving the throwing technique, and getting a better comprehension of how certain discs fly.

Frequent practice and consulting with more seasoned players can make a big difference in progress.

Forehand Throw (Flick):

Another method is the forehand or flick throw, which entails using a sidearm motion while holding the disc with the palm toward the target.

This is a useful toss when you need to go into tight locations or follow a precise flight path, for example.

Method:

A distinct set of abilities, such as wrist control, release timing, and knowledge of disc flight patterns when thrown with a flick action, are needed to master the forehand throw. Gaining expertise in both forehand and backhand throws broadens a player's repertoire of abilities.

When To Apply It:

For strategic play, knowing when to use a forehand throw is essential. It is frequently used when a certain shot shape is needed or when a backhand throw is not feasible because of obstructions. Skilled players can evaluate the course and choose the best throw for each situation.

Throws Overhead:

Throwing the disc overhand is what's meant by advanced techniques such as the thumber and tomahawk. These throws are especially helpful when attempting a steep descent toward the target or when negotiating obstructions like trees.

Finger:

The thumber is an overhand throw in which the thumb and fingers are placed above and below the disc. This throw creates a distinct flight path that frequently has a consistent fade. Gaining proficiency with the thumber broadens a player's toolkit.

Tomahawk:

Another overhand throw that requires holding the disc with fingers on top and thumb underneath is the tomahawk. Compared to the thumber, this throw produces a different spin and flight pattern.

It can be helpful to know when to utilize the tomahawk in certain course circumstances.

Being proficient in all of the disc golf throws and techniques is necessary to develop into a well-rounded player.

Having a strong base in grip, posture, and backhand throw combined with forehand throws and overhead methods improves a player's ability to maneuver around a variety of course layouts.

Consistent practice and comprehension of strategic decision-making enhance one's ability to progress over time and enjoy this demanding and exciting sport.

CHAPTER FIVE

METHODS AND ACTIVITY

With the accuracy of frisbee tossing combined with aspects of traditional golf, disc golf is a dynamic and strategic game. Comprehending and employing efficacious tactics throughout gameplay is a crucial element of being a proficient disc golf player. A mix of talents, such as shot selection, course evaluation, and mental toughness, are frequently used by successful players.

Organizing Your Shots

In disc golf, shot planning is essential since it requires strategic decision-making regarding the layout of the course. Every shot must be planned taking into account variables like the basket's location, wind direction, and topography. Expert players take the time to evaluate distance, stability, and their throwing style when determining the best path to the target and choosing the right disc for the job.

Evaluating the Course

An essential component of disc golf strategy is course assessment. The course layout must be understood by players, as well as possible hazards and throw-advantageous possibilities. Studying the terrain, spotting elevation changes, and paying attention to the placement of trees, bushes, and other objects that may affect shot placement are all necessary for this.

Choose Your Shots

Expert disc golfers stand out for their ability to select the ideal shot in any given circumstance. To ensure a good throw, players must choose the disc with the specific flight characteristics that fit the distance and needed trajectory. For consistently best performance, shot selection must be adapted to the conditions and layout of the course.

A Mental Look at Disc Golf

Disc golf demands a strong cerebral game in addition to physical prowess. A player's mental state has a big impact on their performance as a whole and can make all the difference between winning and losing on the course.

Concentration And Focus

In disc golf, it's imperative to stay focused and attentive during a round. Both internal and external distractions might impair a player's ability to hit shots with accuracy. A mindset that enables them to tune out outside distractions, be present, and concentrate on the task at hand is developed by successful players.

Handling Stress

Disc golfers sometimes find themselves in stressful situations, particularly when competing. It is possible to improve one's ability to handle pressure, whether it be for a crucial putt or a stroke to save par. Effective pressure management involves controlling anxiety, maintaining composure, and having faith in one's talents.

Techniques For Visualization

A lot of disc golfers utilize visualization as a useful technique to improve their game. Players frequently see the disc's trajectory, flight route, and landing spot before making a shot. This mental practice increases the likelihood of successfully performing the targeted shot by helping to create a clear and positive vision. Additionally, visualization techniques can be used to improve mental preparation and general confidence.

Disc golf takes a combination of mental toughness, shot selection, and strategic thinking to succeed. Disc golfers who become proficient in these areas will be better able to handle the course's obstacles and regularly perform well.

CHAPTER SIX

DISC GOLF AREA

The sport of disc golf is expanding quickly and has created a friendly and lively community. Fans congregate to express their love of the game, regardless of age or ability level.

The community places a strong emphasis on friendship, sportsmanship, and a love of nature. Players' common passion for disc golf frequently leads to the formation of enduring friendships.

Competitions And Occasions

Disc golf competitions and events are important to the community because they provide players a chance to compete at different levels and show off their talents.

A new dimension is added to the game when you play in tournaments, regardless of your skill level.

Regional Competitions

The core of the sport is local disc golf competitions, which provide participants a stage to showcase their skills in their local communities. These gatherings frequently welcome participants of all ability levels, encouraging amicable rivalry and community involvement. Local competitions are a great way for new players to get a taste of the excitement of structured play.

Events Of The Professional Disc Golf Association (PDGA)

Playing in the Professional Disc Golf Association (PDGA) competition is a crucial step for anyone wishing to advance in their disc golf career. International and regional competitions are governed and sanctioned by the PDGA. These competitions draw elite players, providing viewers and competitors with an opportunity to see disc golf at its highest level.

Getting Involved In Disc Golf

Getting involved in a disc golf club is a great opportunity to meet others who share your interests and to get more involved in the sport. Clubs give players a safe space to exchange advice, tactics, and life lessons. Joining a club also makes it possible to take part in tournaments and activities that are planned.

Advantages

Disc golf has several advantages for the body and mind. In addition to providing cardiovascular activity, the sport challenges players' minds with accuracy and strategy.

Regular disc golf play can enhance focus, coordination, and endurance.

 Disc golf courses' outdoor environment also offers players a revitalizing chance to get outside and take in the scenery.

Locating Neighborhood Clubs

It's usually easy to find local disc golf clubs by contacting the disc golf community online or by contacting the parks and recreation agencies in your area. A lot of clubs are active on social media, which facilitates communication for new members. In addition to improving your disc golfing experience, joining a club connects you to a community of like-minded players who can guide you through the local disc golf scene.

Disc golf is a social pastime that attracts players from many walks of life, not just athletes. There is a place for everyone in the disc golf community, regardless of whether you play for fun on the weekends or want to compete at the top level. Take advantage of the many mental and physical health advantages that come with this thrilling and easily accessible activity by embracing camaraderie, competing in events, and thinking about joining a club.

CHAPTER SEVEN

FITNESS AND SUITABILITY

Playing disc golf is a sport that calls for both mental and physical stamina. Because players move in a variety of ways, including walking, jogging, and throwing, it's critical to keep up general conditioning and fitness. Strength training and cardiovascular exercises are examples of regular exercise that might help you perform better on the disc golf course. Exercises for flexibility are also advantageous since they improve the range of motion needed for successful throws.

Benefits Of Disc Golf For Your Body

Playing disc golf has several physical advantages. The activity improves endurance and cardiovascular health by having participants walk long distances across a variety of terrains. Furthermore, throwing the disc works a variety of muscle groups, which enhances strength and muscle tone. The outside environment of disc golf exposes players to sunlight and fresh air, improving general well-being and possibly lowering stress levels.

Warm-Up Before The Game

In disc golf, as in any other sport, it is imperative to warm up properly before play. By preparing the muscles for the physical demands of the game, warming up helps lower the chance of injury. A thorough warm-up regimen could involve dynamic stretching, mild running, and targeted disc-throwing exercises. By boosting blood flow to the muscles and enhancing joint flexibility, taking the time to warm up properly can improve performance.

Injury Avoidance

Because disc golf involves such dynamic movements, injury avoidance is an important part of the game. To reduce strain on their joints and muscles, athletes should concentrate on maintaining correct throwing mechanics. Injuries can also be avoided by utilizing the proper equipment, such as discs that are appropriate for a player's skill level and style of play. Incorporating cross-training exercises and getting enough rest in between rounds can also help reduce the risk of injury.

Typical Injuries

Disc golf does carry some risk of injury despite its comparatively low-impact nature. Strains or sprains in the shoulders, elbows, or wrists are common ailments that are sometimes brought on by incorrect throwing technique or overexertion.

To prevent overuse injuries, players should pay attention to their form and pay attention to their bodies. Furthermore, minor injuries might result from slips or falls on uneven terrain, underscoring the significance of playing with situational awareness.

Healing And Rehabilitative Care

In the event of an injury, getting well and recovering quickly is necessary to get back on the disc golf course. The conventional techniques for treating acute injuries are rest, ice, compression, and elevation, or RICE. A safe recovery process can be aided by rehabilitation activities and consulting a medical practitioner. To prevent re-injury, players should focus on gradually reintroducing activities rather than jumping back into the game too quickly.

Disc golf-specific rehabilitation exercises help address imbalances or weaknesses that may be contributing factors to injury.

Disc golf is a physically demanding sport that also requires mental and emotional preparation. Players can enjoy the game while reducing the risk of injuries and optimizing their overall performance and well-being by realizing the significance of warm-ups, injury prevention, and appropriate recovery.

CHAPTER EIGHT

DISC GOLF: HISTORY AND CULTURE

With the accuracy and skill of throwing a disc combined with aspects of traditional golf, disc golf has become a very popular sport in recent years. Disc golf is a community sport that is based on outdoor appreciation, inclusivity, and companionship. Disc golf's history began with the establishment of its first official courses in the 1960s, which launched a sport that has since spread over the world.

Disc Golf's Evolution

The invention of flying discs, also referred to as Frisbees, had a significant influence on the creation of disc golf. Throwing flying discs at targets was formerly only a fun hobby for friends, but it eventually developed into an official sport. Standardized rules and regulations were initially created in 1975 when the first official disc golf course was built in Pasadena,

California. With the evolution of disc designs over time, players today use a spectrum of discs designed specifically for different facets of the game, such as putters, mid-ranges, and drivers.

Leading Persons In Disc Golf

Many well-known people who have made substantial contributions to the development and popularity of disc golf have come from the sport.

Ken Climo, sometimes known as the "Champ," is one such person who dominated the disc golf scene in the 1990s and early 2000s, winning multiple titles and establishing the bar for other players to follow.

Paul McBeth, a disc golf superstar of today who has won numerous world championships, is another significant figure.

These individuals, among numerous others, have significantly influenced the development of disc golf competition.

Worldwide Distribution And Adolescence

Disc golf has grown from a niche activity to a global sensation, with courses located on every continent. The appeal of the sport is due to its accessibility, low cost, and the welcoming atmosphere of the disc golf community. Disc golf is an adaptable and generally accessible recreational activity that can be found in urban parks, rural settings, and even mountainous terrain. The sport has grown even more as a result of regional, national, and worldwide competitions that draw athletes of all abilities.

Disc golf's international community is proof of the sport's enduring appeal as it continues to gain popularity. Disc golf is a popular pastime for people of all ages and backgrounds because it provides a special combination of athleticism, strategy, and outdoor enjoyment, whether it is played competitively at a professional level or just for fun with friends.

FINAL VERDICT

Disc golf is a community that is growing and a means of personal development, not just a game. Along with honing their abilities, players who complete courses join a wider community that celebrates the fun of the game and the relationships made there. For people of all ages and backgrounds, disc golf is an exciting and approachable sport because of its unique blend of strategy, athleticism, and social interaction.

Summary Of The Main Ideas

A range of discs are used to travel courses in disc golf, which is a game with basic rules and gameplay components. The variety of the course layout, which includes both open fields and wooded regions, enhances the playing experience. Players always work to improve their skills, honing their methods and approaches as they go. Players can enjoy the game and build enduring relationships in this welcoming environment thanks to the community's support and inclusive culture.

Motivation To Keep Improving

A dedication to ongoing development is essential for players hoping to get the most out of their disc golfing experience. Refining abilities and strengthening one's bond with the sport can be accomplished through frequent practice, consulting with seasoned players, and attending local competitions. Long-term success and happiness in disc golf are influenced by accepting the learning process, appreciating little accomplishments, and remaining receptive to new experiences.

Disc Golf's Future In Perspective

With increased participation and funding, disc golf looks to have a bright future. The community is probably going to grow as new courses are created and competitions become more well-known. Digital platforms and live streaming are examples of technological innovations that give spectators new opportunities to interact with the sport. To guarantee disc golf's success and further development in the years to come, it will be imperative that players, course designers, and disc golf organizations continue to work together.

Printed in the USA
CPSIA information can be obtained
at www.ICGtesting.com
CBHW062258110924
14439CB00007B/313